The Full Extent of His Love
A Lenten Devotional Study

Heather Grant Harrison

Dedicated to my Study and Savor group.
You are often the first readers of my thoughts.
It is a joy to walk through Scripture with you.

Table of Contents

Before we begin…

In a world where every moment is fully of activity, taking time to pause might feel out of context but is vital for the flourishing of our souls. The fact that you are holding this book indicates you, like me, need the restoration and respite found in Jesus Christ. I'm thrilled to take this much needed time of preparation with you.

If you're in a more liturgical tradition, you're probably familiar with Lent, but if not, this season might be new to you. Lent is a time to help us focus on Jesus. Similar to how Advent can help us prepare for the birth of Christ, Lent is a time to set our sights on His resurrection.

This 40 day season (from Ash Wednesday to Easter, not counting Sundays) is set aside to reflect, remember, and prepare.
We **reflect** on who God is and who we are in His sight.
We **remember** all He's done and is doing in us and around us.
We **prepare** our hearts for Him and for what He has for us.

Why 40? Because 40 is a significant number throughout Scripture signifying a time of testing, trial, judgment, or preparation.

Jesus spent 40 days in the wilderness in preparation for ministry. There were 40 days between Jesus' resurrection and His ascension. Moses was on Mount Sinai for 40 days and nights.

The three pillars of Lent are typically Fasting, Prayer, and Giving. We'll talk a bit about each of those in the coming weeks, but I want to bring them up now to encourage you to consider how you might incorporate them into your own personal time.

What might you lay aside in order to focus on the Lord? Whether a type of food, activity, or habit, is there something you're feeling a nudge to lay down?

Is there a way to create more margin in your life during this time so you can spend time in prayer?

What is God calling you to give--time, money, effort, etc—as a response to what He has graciously given you?

As you think about our season of preparation, consider the following questions. Jot down your thoughts in response to the ones that resonate with you.

.

What does preparation mean and how can I prepare for Jesus and what He is doing?

What do I want to set aside and what do I want to add into my daily or weekly rhythms in order to create space for God to move?

As I plan to spend more time in prayer, is there a specific focus? (personally, for a loved one, the world)

How would I like this season to affect me, and how would I like it to affect those around me?

Keep in mind, all of these are done to prepare and make space for what the Lord is doing in you and around you. I encourage you to sit with these questions, asking God for His thoughts. Your answers to these questions are between you and the Lord, but if you decide you want to set aside something that is a habit or addiction in your life, reach out to someone for support.

Pour Out Your Heart / Day 1

As we walk together toward the cross and then to the empty tomb, I'm convinced God has something for us, but it begins with taking an honest look at ourselves and our world.

Ash Wednesday is a somber reminder of human mortality and the need for reconciliation with God, beckoning us to take a look at "what is" and "what will be."

It is appropriate to mourn that our world is not how it was created to be. It is appropriate to mourn that our own lives are not without struggle, sadness, suffering, and sin.

Several weeks ago, we gathered with our small group to pray for all that is happening in our world. We prayed about all the current issues, we prayed for loved ones who were struggling, and we prayed for each other. There were many tears from the men and women in that room as we cried out to God.

Scripture calls this vocal mourning "Lament."

Lament is a passionate expression of grief or sorrow. Lament is crying out to God. Lament is pouring out our hearts to God because we see the discrepancy between His heart and our world. We lament the way things are around us or inside us, while clinging to the character and heart of God. The difference between lament and angry complaint is that the first remembers His goodness, and the second doubts His goodness.

The hope of Easter takes us a step further: as we mourn how things are, we do so with the hope that things are not how they will be. From personal struggle to relational conflict, from sickness and death to global turmoil: we can face the reality of what is with courage and with hope, because we know this isn't the final act in God's grand story.

So we do what Psalm 62:8 tells us to do:

pour out your heart to Him, for God is our refuge

We pour out our hearts to Him because He is our refuge. It doesn't say "pour out your heart because God will make your life comfortable, say yes to your every wish, or help you live your best life now."

We pour because life is hard, and because He can be trusted. He is a safe place to leave the contents of our hearts and minds, AND He is the One who can answer and transform.

We pour because His thoughts toward us don't shift depending on what we tell Him. His love doesn't wane. He doesn't get uncomfortable when we "overshare." His love and care for His own does not dissipate but endures. When it feels like everything else is dried up, we look to find that God's love remains. His love for us has already been decided and determined. It has nothing to do with our personality, actions, family history, or dignified prayers, but has everything to do with our belief and trust in Him. When we lament the suffering around us or pour out our personal struggle to Him, there is no confusion who the faithful, powerful, omniscient One is.

This week, pour out your heart, lament, cry out to your loving Father. It is in the pouring out that we bring our real selves to Him, not a calculated façade. As we do this, He works through, not in spite of, our vulnerability to transform us from grace to grace and from glory to glory.

*One more thing about ashes.

Ashes are a source of lime and potassium and other elements that many plants need to thrive and are often used as a fertilizer for new growth.

As we pour out our hearts to Him this week, we can remember that not only does He give beauty for ashes (Is.61:3), He even uses the very ashes of our lament to nourish and spring forth new life in us and in our world.

So on this day, we pause and remember our humanity. We remember that we are not the exalted one…and we turn our attention to Him who is.

Take your time as you read the following Scriptures. Consider, journal, or discuss the questions.

Lamentations 3: 22-26 In an entire book filled with lament, why is it significant that these verses are tucked in the midst of it all?

Psalm 13 What do you notice about the difference between how this Psalm begins and how it ends? What causes this?

We Wait / Day 2

We wait in hope for the Lord; He is our help and our shield.
In Him our hearts rejoice, for we trust in His holy name.
May your unfailing love rest upon us, O Lord,
even as we put our hope in You.
Psalm 33:20-22

Often, the glare from a busy life can blind us to reality, causing us to forfeit deep meaning and true life for one that skims the surface in pursuit of ease and comfort. During this season leading up to our celebration of the resurrection, we want to pause, slow down, and wait. We do this because we know it is in the waiting that God often does the deeper soul-work we desire.

We wait. We may wait patiently or we may learn patience along the way, but we wait. We may wait quietly or with shouts, but still we wait.

We hope. We hope, not for what we can see, but for that which remains in the not yet. We hope for the unseen, for hope that is seen is no hope at all.

We trust. We trust in His holy name--in all that He is. We trust a faithful God who has proven Himself. We trust Him with our hearts, our very lives, because He does not disappoint.

We pray, we beg, we pour out, we lament.

We lay our longings at the feet of a good God, and we wait for the time when our desires and His purposes intersect.

When our questions overshadow trust, we give our questioning hearts to Him--this God who walked and sneezed and cried and died and LIVES, this God who put on flesh to save us from our unbelief.

When we dance with doubt and mistake impatience for a friend, He makes up the difference and all the while is changing our heart, aligning it with His own.

When we are shocked as the brokenness below the surface is revealed, we look closer and find Him there, already knowing the depths of our soul, already refining and restoring. Although we are just getting acquainted with our weakness, He knew the extent of it before we took our first breath. He knew He would be our Great Substitute before we knew Him. He knew He would be The Source of our ability to wait and hope and trust.

While we wait, we see the banner of these words, wanting them to be our own:

Yes, Lord, walking in the way of Your truth, Your name and renown are the desire of our hearts.

But when this declaration would be a lie, when we want answers more than we want Him, we ask Him to refine this self-focused, short-sighted heart of ours, and that He wouldn't relent until our heart reflects His.

So we wait, we hope, and we trust, with the strength and joy that He gives, for the time when He is our deepest longing and His glory is our one desire.

Read the following Scriptures and consider each question.

Ecclesiastes 3:1-8, 11, 20 The concept of "seasons" has been around since the beginning, yet for our lives, it is sometimes hard to embrace...why is that? Verse 11 speaks of God's beauty and eternity: how do these two things help you when you are in a hard season of waiting on the Lord?

Psalm 130 Why is pouring out our hearts to the Lord sometimes hard to do? Why is waiting on Him so difficult? What have you found that helps you wait on Him?

Turn Around / Day 3

I was driving to my hometown when I was in college. I was so busy listening to Alanis or Sheryl that I didn't realize I had gone the wrong direction. I finally looked around and noticed nothing looked familiar. I called my mom on my bag phone, and since she worked with the police department, she put an officer on the phone.

"What mile marker do you see?" he asked.

I told him.

"You're in Oklahoma. Turn around."

And he patiently talked me back home.

(For reference, both my hometown and my college were in Arkansas.)

Unfortunately, this is only one of many stories of my poor sense of direction. I get lost all the time!

...

While you probably don't have to turn around as much as I do, I wonder if this happens to many of us spiritually:

we live distracted or absorbed in something other than the spiritual reality of our life, and whether we've made choices in full-blown rebellion, or in neglecting what's most important, or something in between, we need to hear the cry that runs throughout Scripture:

Turn around.

Scripture calls this turning around, "repentance." Many times, when we think of or hear "repent," the message is simply "turn away from sin," but that stops short of the best part, which is: turn to the Lord.

Repentance involves a literal turning away from one thing and turning to another.

How does your body react when you hear the word "repent?" For me, I often bristle at the word and sometimes even get defensive at the suggestion.

When you think of repentance, do you usually think solely of rejecting sin or do you also including turning to God?

We'll flesh this out more in the coming days, but today...

Write this simple question down: Lord, what do I need to turn from and instead turn toward you?

Don't worry if an answer doesn't come right away or if more answers come than you have room to write down. We'll get to that tomorrow.

Today, meditate on the singular idea: Turn Around.

Spend some time in the passage below. What stands out to you?

Acts 3:18-20 *But this is how God fulfilled what he had foretold through all the prophets, saying that his Messiah would suffer. Repent, then, and turn to God, so that your sins may be wiped out, that times of refreshing may come from the Lord, and that he may send the Messiah, who has been appointed for you—even Jesus.*

In Repentance & Rest / Day 4

Isaiah 30:15 *This is what the Sovereign Lord, the Holy One of Israel, says: "In repentance and rest is your salvation, in quietness and trust is your strength, but you would have none of it.*
After talking yesterday about "turning," I want to flesh that out a bit more over the next few days...

"In repentance and rest is your salvation" has always stuck with me. It isn't about taking a break or getting a nap, but a call to turn away from sin and rebellion (repentance) And a call to turn from trusting our own works (rest) in an attempt to be acceptable to God. Hebrews 4 teaches that we must stop trying to be made right by our own goodness, actions, and good works, and instead we must "rest" from our self-work and trust in Christ's work. This doesn't mean we are idle, but that our trust is placed in Christ alone, and not in ourselves or our own merit.

In repentance –turning from rebellion – *is your salvation*

In rest – turning from your self-righteousness – *is your salvation*

Yesterday we read that one thread throughout Scripture is "turn around."

Turn around:

Resist and leave behind that which binds you, makes false promises, and prevents God's best.

Turn away:

From your own goodness and from trusting your actions to justify you before the Lord.

Turn to:

…Your Father, your Abba, who called you and is calling you now,

…Jesus, your brother, Savior, King who sacrificially accomplished your entrance into the family of God,

…The Spirit who woos, comforts, convicts, and heals.

Turn your affection, your eyes, your hands, your life to the One who forgives, heals, loves, and calls you to walk through this life with Him and for Him. Turn your face to Him.

.

Spend some time in Isaiah 30:15.

Write a prayer to the Lord in response to His invitation to turn to Him and away from other things.

Sunday / Remember and Worship

Today is about responding to what the Lord has shown you this week. Take time to review your notes and ask the Lord how He'd have you respond. He is such a faithful Shepherd. Notice in the passage below how responding to the Lord is followed by Him showing us more of Himself. That is our prayer for the coming week.

Proverbs 1:7, 23 *The fear of the Lord is the beginning of knowledge, but fools despise wisdom and instruction… Repent at my rebuke! Then I will pour out my thoughts to you, I will make known to you my teachings.*

Let's continue the thought of "turning around" by taking a look at another life-changing aspect…

As you read the two verses from Isaiah 41 below, picture what's described in your mind…

Isaiah 41:10, 13 So do not fear, for I am with you, so do not be dismayed, for I am your God. I will strengthen you and help you; I will uphold you with my righteous right hand…

…For I am the Lord, your God who **takes hold of your right hand **and says to you "do not fear; I will help you."

The Father, holding His child with His righteous right hand-- the hand of power and salvation--then takes hold of the child's right hand. Can you picture it?

Being held with His right hand while He's holding the child's right hand puts them face to face. The child is facing the Father. He is holding the child close. Face to face...whispering, "do not fear, I will help you."

Friends, your Father in heaven upholds you with His hand of great power, all while holding your right hand, drawing you close, face to face, whispering words of comfort and hope.

He calls each of us to turn away from other loves and to turn to Him, face to face, held close. In fact, He invites us to live our lives face to face with Him.

Read the Scriptures below while holding this question before the Lord:

"What does "face to face living" look like in my life? How does that affect me?

Numbers 6:24-26: *The Lord bless you and keep you; the Lord make his face shine on you and be gracious to you; the Lord turn his face toward you and give you peace.*

1 Corinthians 13:12 *Now we see but a poor reflection as in a mirror; then we shall see face to face. Now I know in part; then I shall know fully, even as I am fully known.*

Search Me, Oh God / Day 6

Search me, God, and know my heart; test me and know my anxious thoughts. See if there is any offensive way in me, and lead me in the way everlasting. Psalm 139: 23-24

Since Genesis 3, God's children have been caught in a cycle of sin and shame. And just as He did then, He still seeks them out asking "Where are you?"

When we live "face to face" with Him, hiding in shame no longer needs to be our response when we mess up. We don't have to pay a penance or stay away long enough until He's not mad anymore, because, just as He made provision for them in the garden by covering them with a slain animal, He has also covered us with His Son, the slain Lamb of God.

This doesn't mean sin isn't a big deal, after all it cost His Son His life. It does mean that since the price for sin is paid, we cannot by our shame, add to that payment. We will never be able to add our blood, sweat, or tears to the payment already paid. It is finished. Finished.

What, then, is the role of repentance in the life of His blood-bought children?

We know He is transforming us, changing us from the inside out so let's walk through the process together....

Conviction is usually where we begin. This is not condemnation which is from the enemy and declares you are condemned. Conviction is when the Holy Spirit pinpoints an area of sin in our life for the purpose of restoration. It's as if the Spirit says, "that's not for you anymore."

After conviction, we can either resist what God is doing or we can confess:

"Father forgive me for _____. I give it over to you."

This is where we begin. We agree with Him about any sin or brokenness or weakness in our life. We confess it to Him, and in that agreement comes a unique power to go from vocal confession to literal life change.

How does long lasting change happen? Does He simply give us the ability to never envy, gossip, lust, etc again? Or is He more involved in the process of our transformation?

Let's use something that may be common to a lot of us: envy.

After we recognize and confess to Him, He begins to show us the envy for what it is, its ugliness, and how it has invaded more of our heart than we first thought. We begin to see that sin is not simply one singular action, but an all-out resistance to who He is and what He's doing. He shows us what we are wanting and seeking when we are envious...

When I'm envious, it's because--

I want to be seen

I want to be known

I want to be admired

I want to be comfortable

This doesn't mean we focus on our sin, but that He is interested in changing us from the inside out. Sure, He wants outward change, but that must first be coupled with inward transformation. When we come to Him and confess, He gives us His eyesight and shows us where it comes from and then (this is the best part) shows me how those desires are misplaced and will only be satisfied in Him.

He sees me

He knows me

He adores me and shows me how to adore Him

He comforts me

When we live our lives in Christ instead of hiding in shame, we have the intimate freedom to bring our whole selves to Him. We bring our sin in repentance, and we can also do this same prayer process with our weaknesses or insecurities because we know He desires radical, inner transformation.

Here's another beautiful part of this—we can turn to Him in confession over and over, and we'll begin to see that what the enemy meant for our destruction has actually caused us to spend the day with the Father.

And that, my friend, changes everything.

I'd love for you to work through this process today.

Here's an example prayer to walk through.

"Father forgive me for _____. I give it over to you."

Lord, help me to see _____ as you see it.

Lord, where does this come from? What am I seeking from this? How do You meet those desires or needs?

Are there Scriptures that help you understand how He is sufficient to meet your misplaced desires?

Deliver Me, Oh God / Day 7

What a beautiful design and promise that God will forgive, deliver, and restore us. We can walk away from the "try harder" life and embrace the grace and power He gives. We can bring our sin and struggle to Him, and in exchange, He will pour out His goodness and strength.

Read the lyrics of I Shall Not Want by Audrey Assad below.

From the love of my own comfort
From the fear of having nothing
From a life of worldly passions
Deliver me O God
From the need to be understood
And from a need to be accepted
From the fear of being lonely
Deliver me O God
Deliver me O God
And I shall not want, no, I shall not want
When I taste Your goodness, I shall not want
When I taste Your goodness, I shall not want
From the fear of serving others
Oh, and from the fear of death or trial
And from the fear of humility
Deliver me O God
Yes, deliver me O God
And I shall not want, no, I shall not want
When I taste Your goodness I shall not want
No, I shall not want, no, I shall not want
When I taste Your goodness I shall not want
When I taste Your goodness I shall not want
I shall not want
I shall not want

Prayerfully, make your own "deliver me" list:

From _____, deliver me, Oh God.

From _____, deliver me, Oh God…

You can find her beautiful song online as well.

Read Psalm 23 and consider: How does knowing the Lord is your shepherd affect your heart? How does knowing Him in this way impact your daily life?

Psalm 23

The Lord is my shepherd, I shall not want.

He makes me lie down in green pastures,

He leads me beside quiet waters, He restores my soul.

He guides me along the right paths for His name's sake.

Even though I walk through the valley of death,

I will fear no evil, for You are with me;

Your rod and your staff, they comfort me.

You prepare a table before me in the presence of my enemies.

You anoint my head with oil; my cup overflows.

Surely Your goodness and love will follow me all the days of my life, and I will dwell in the house of the Lord forever.

Mercy / Day 8

You may have heard these definitions of grace and mercy: grace is God giving us what we don't deserve; mercy is God withholding what we do deserve.

When God "withholds what we deserve" and show us mercy, it isn't because He's blind to our sin, and it isn't because He's decided sin is ok. God hates sin and there's never a time He deems it good. If you want to know God's heart towards sin, read the Old Testament or look at the cross. A holy God cannot call evil good.

When we say God is merciful, it is a conscious decision on His part to see us through the lens of the cross. The reason Jesus came was to do what we couldn't do–pay for our sin and rescue us from its oppression. Scripture says He remembers we are dust: He knows what's in us. Do we bear His image? We do. But this doesn't negate sin's effect on us, it adds weight to the heaviness of it: God's image bearers have chosen a different way.

God not only knows about our sin, waywardness, and brokenness - He also knows the intricate details of it - the hidden motives, the origin and reasons for it, the darkness of it. He knows our heart, including our sin, better than we do.

Along with that thorough knowledge, He also knows the cross would pay for it and the resurrection would render it temporary and ineffective in the life of His own.
Sin has been fought and defeated, and you and I can live in Jesus' ultimate and final victory, even though we are still

living in the time before that victory is in our view.
But God already sees the victory.

Is sin costly? It is. It cost God incarnate, the Author of Life, His very life.

For us to look through His merciful eye, it doesn't mean we see a thief or murderer and think, "it's ok, it's not that bad." But we know that the same mercy we live in is available to them. We know if God didn't see through His lens of mercy, I couldn't stand and neither could you. We know that the difference between the thief and me is that his greed is full-grown and mine was interrupted by the cross of Christ.

And that interruption has changed everything.

Our focus isn't on our sin, because that's not who we are anymore. Yes, the work of Christ was that effective and powerful! We no longer live wallowing in who we were, but in who He is making us into, because in His great love, that's who He sees when He looks at us. We live with gratefulness and vibrant confidence, not because we didn't need a Savior, but because that Savior's blood had such a far-reaching, down-in-the-depths effect.

Jesus saw and sees through mercy, not because He's unaware of the depth of sin, but because He knows full well the power of His blood. Your sin, my sin, "their" sin is great? His blood is greater. How silly for Jesus to come for the purpose of redemption but despise those who needed it.

His withholding of what we deserve would have been enough wouldn't it? But like He always does, He goes beyond what was enough and in addition to mercy, He pours out grace upon grace. Incredible.

When you and I grasp just how much mercy we've received, giving mercy to another is a no-brainer.

Who am I to withhold what's been freely given to me?

Draw a picture or write a prayer, song, or poem in response to our merciful God.

A New Heart and New Spirit / Day 9

When we begin to see what Christ calls us away from and what He calls us to, we can move forward in our own efforts, or we can walk in the power of the Spirit. If you're like me, you've probably experienced both (maybe even within the same hour!).

Living the life He calls us to and living out the holiness He is working in us, requires the Spirit. Otherwise, our lives might look ok on the outside without true heart change on the inside, replacing one self-focused way for another more acceptable self-focused way.

Read the passage below and answer the question that follows.

Ezekiel 36:25-27 *I will sprinkle clean water on you, and you will be clean; I will cleanse you from all your impurities and from all your idols. I will give you a new heart and put a new spirit in you; I will remove from you your heart of stone and give you a heart of flesh. And I will put my Spirit in you and move you to follow my decrees and be careful to keep my laws.*

Where have you embraced true heart change and where have you simply been trying hard to change?

Gifts From Above / Day 10

Our journey together through Lent is one of preparation. We know Good Friday and Easter are coming, so making space in our lives to receive what the Lord has to give us is not just a good idea, but is needed to fully receive, learn, and grow in Him.

As we said early on in our time together, the three pillars of Lent are typically prayer, fasting, and giving. We spent the first week of our time looking at prayer and what it means to pour our hearts out to the Lord; and we spent last week looking at what we want to turn from and instead turn to the Lord. In the coming week we're going to focus on giving. Let's begin by remembering what God has given us.

Have you paused lately to answer the question, "what has God given to me?"

Read the Scripture below and then make a list with the title, "God has given me…,"

James 1:17 Every good and perfect gift is from above, coming down from the Father of the heavenly lights, who does not change like shifting shadows.

God has given me:

Sunday / Worship and Respond

Today is about responding to what the Lord has shown you this week. Take time to review your notes and ask the Lord how He'd have you respond. Write out the Scriptures that have been most meaningful and commit them to memory.

Giving and Receiving / Day 11

Never ending and countless. Those are the two words that come to mind when I think of the question from Saturday, "what has God given me?" If we believe that every good gift is from His hand, we can start by naming all the "good things" in our lives, but then we quickly begin to think of all the things that aren't "things" as well: joy, love, forgiveness…and as our list grows, other things come to mind: like the time we almost wrecked but didn't, or the time we found ourselves in a sticky situation and somehow came out unscathed….

In the midst of reflecting on all He's given, we remember the words of Acts 20:35: *It is more blessed to give than receive.*

As wonderful as it is to receive, it is far better to give. I agree with this, but as I look at my life, I notice it doesn't always look like I believe it.

This week, as we discuss giving, ask God to share His generous heart with you.

If it truly is better to give than to get, why are we sometimes so hesitant to give? Have you noticed this in your life? What does it mean that it's better to give than receive?

Oh Lord, cause our hearts to overflow with gratefulness, resulting in generosity to others. Help us to see how abundant your grace, love, and provisions have been in our lives and in response, change us from the inside out.

Open the Floodgates / Day 12

In light of what we read yesterday, that it is better to give than receive, how about a challenge?

For the rest of the week, find a way each day to give in an unexpected way and let's see what happens. Since our giving should be done as secretly as possible, don't share what you do each day with anyone.

Here are some ways you can give each day, but I know you will have even more ideas:

Give to a local or global charity

Send an encouraging text

Pay for a friend's lunch

Take coffee to someone

Write a note

Give unexpected grace

Spend extra time in prayer for someone else

Cancel a debt

I've heard before that "you can't outgive God." I absolutely agree with this, however, I think sometimes this is mistakenly interpreted that if we give our money, He'll cause us to win the lottery!

Does God supply our needs? Yes.

Does He give us good gifts? Also yes.

But often the way God "outgives" us is not in ways we might think.

So as we look for ways to give this week, also keep your eyes alert to the ways God "outgives" you. We can't manipulate God by our giving, but we do know that we will never be more generous than He is. What a beautiful truth that our generous God also shows us how to be generous with others.

Sit with the Scripture below asking God to sanctify your heart away from greed and toward generosity.

Malachi 3:10 *Bring the whole tithe into the storehouse, that there may be food in my house. Test me in this," says the Lord Almighty, "and see if I will not throw open the floodgates of heaven and pour out so much blessing that there will not be room enough to store it.*

The Earth is the Lord's / Day 13

Do you have people in your life that are impossible to buy gifts for? Have you figured this out or have you, like me, started giving gift cards? Seriously, what do you give someone who has everything?!

Similarly, what do you give to God, who owns all things. And not only owns all things, but created all things, including you and me? What do you give Someone who has everything?!

What do we give to God?

Over the next few days, we'll look at Scriptures each day that helps inform what and why we give to God. The first ones are below.

Psalm 24:1-2 *The earth is the Lord's, and everything in it, the world, and all who live in it; for he founded it on the seas and established it on the waters.*

Psalm 50:9-15 *I have no need of a bull from your stall or of goats from your pens, for every animal of the forest is mine, and the cattle on a thousand hills.I know every bird in the mountains, and the insects in the fields are mine. If I were hungry I would not tell you, for the world is mine, and all that is in it. Do I eat the flesh of bulls or drink the blood of goats? "Sacrifice thank offerings to God, fulfill your vows to the Most High, and call on me in the day of trouble, I will deliver you, and you will honor me."*

What do you learn from these passages?

If you're taking the challenge we discussed yesterday, also spend time in prayer asking Him, "Lord, what would you have me give today?"

A Living Sacrifice / Day 14

Yesterday, we read that everything is the Lord's; He has no needs. This leads to the question: What do we give Him?

Let's look at a Scripture in Romans to learn…

Romans 12:1-2 *Therefore, I urge you, brothers and sisters, in view of God's mercy, to offer your bodies as a living sacrifice, holy and pleasing to God—this is your true and proper worship.*

In view of His great mercy ->offer your bodies as a living sacrifice=this is worship.

We live our lives to, for, and through Him. We give our entire selves to Him. This is how we worship.

Consider another Scripture:

Psalm 51:15-17 *Open my lips, Lord, and my mouth will declare your praise. You do not delight in sacrifice, or I would bring it; you do not take pleasure in burnt offerings. My sacrifice, O God, is a broken spirit; a broken and contrite heart you, God, will not despise.*

We give praise.

We give a humble heart.

We exalt Him and bow low.

So, what do we give to God? The ironic answer is this:

We give God everything…

Not because He needs it, and not because He requires it to secure our position with Him, but we give Him everything because He's worth it. Our "giving" to God is a response to who He is and what He's done. When we give to God, we're declaring that all we have is already His and from His hand. Giving is good for us because it actually does loosen our grip. In His generosity, God gives us many things, but it's when we white knuckle those gifts and tether our heart to them instead of to Him, that we allow those things to take a place in our lives they were never intended to. We hold His gifts loosely and we give our whole selves back to Him…

Look back through the passages above, continuing to ask God to share His generous heart with you.

What does offering yourselves as a living sacrifice to God look like in your life? Take time to journal or discuss your thoughts with a friend.

Tomorrow we'll look at the question: "If God doesn't need anything, but calls us to give ourselves to Him, where does giving to others come in?"

Good Works / Day 15

"God doesn't need your good works, but your neighbor does." Martin Luther

Spend time in the Scriptures below. What do you learn about giving to others?

Mark 10:45 *For even the Son of Man did not come to be served, but to serve, and to give his life as a ransom for many."*

Mark 12:30-31 *Love the Lord your God with all your heart and with all your soul and with all your mind and with all your strength. 'The second is this: 'Love your neighbor as yourself.' No other commandment is greater than these.*

Luke 12:48 *From everyone who has been given much, much will be demanded; and from the one who has been entrusted with much, much more will be asked.*

Lord, show us your heart for us and for others. Lord share your heart with us.

In light of the quote, these Scriptures, and our "giving challenge," what can you do these last two days of our "giving week" that gives God's goodness to your neighbor?

Open Your Hands / Day 16

Let's remember what we've been reading and learning this week:

God doesn't "need" us or anything we have

And yet…

He calls us to give ourselves and all that we are to Him. Why? Because He's worth it, and because that's what we were made for. As we give ourselves, we experience Him in a deeper way.

He calls us to serve and give to others. Why? Because that's the method He's decided to use to share His love with people, and as we collaborate with Him in this way, we experience Him in a deeper way.

We've asked, "what does 'face to face' living look like?"

Let's now consider open handed living.

Even if they are clenched around good things, clenched hands are attached and bound nonetheless. Open hands are free to give and free to receive.

Consider these questions:

What does 'open-handed' living look like?

What does it require?

What are the benefits?

What are the difficulties or pitfalls?

What Scriptures come to mind?

Lord, all I have is yours.

When my hands are open, I can show Your love in tangible, more-than-enough, over-the-top ways.

When my hands are open, I exchange greed for generosity.

When my hands are open, I can give whatever you prompt me to give.

When my hands are open, I no longer have to negotiate or manipulate.

When my hands are open, I can surrender my plans and embrace Yours.

When my hands are open, I am ready to receive whatever You have.

When my hands are open, I am ready to receive You.

Sunday / Remember and Worship

Today is about responding to what the Lord has shown you this week. Take time to review your notes and ask the Lord how He'd have you respond. What has God shown you in regard to His generosity?

I AM / Day 17

This week we are going to spend our time reading and absorbing the 7 "I am" statements of Jesus.

I AM. The first-century Jewish listener would have known these words. They would have been familiar as they heard the stories of Moses recounted over and over.

The Great I AM, the self-existent God...these words would have brought back a rush of memory and meaning like a scene from a movie when someone is brought rapidly back into consciousness. The burning bush, the holy ground, the questions, the answer. The Answer. The I Am.

"What if they ask 'what is His name' what should I tell them? I am. Tell them 'The Lord, the God of your fathers—the God of Abraham, the God of Isaac and the God of Jacob—has sent me to you.' This is my name forever, the name you shall call me from generation to generation." Exodus 3:13-15

Who is He? What is His name?

He is I am. He is the God of your forefathers, the One who made a covenant with His people. The One who always was, always is, and always will be.

As Charles John Ellicott says in his commentary, "'I am' cannot be declared in words, nor can it be conceived of by human thought. He exists in such a sort that His whole inscrutable nature is implied in His existence. He exists, as nothing else does--necessarily, eternally, really."

When we turn several pages and progress through 'generation to generation, we find Jesus using these same words to describe Himself.

Imagine the sound of these words coming from the Humble Carpenter as He declares, "I AM..."

Spend some time in Exodus 3 today to prepare for our week.

What stands out to you from this chapter?

The Bread of Life / Day 18

"Very truly I tell you, it is not Moses who has given you the bread from heaven, but it is my Father who gives you the true bread from heaven. For the bread of God is the bread that comes down from heaven and gives life to the world."

"Sir," they said, "always give us this bread." Then Jesus declared, "I am the bread of life. Whoever comes to me will never go hungry, and whoever believes in me will never be thirsty." John 6:32-35

Jesus had just fed 5,000+ people using 5 loaves of bread and 2 small fish. After the disciples distributed this miraculous food, they carried away 12 baskets full of bread. They hop in a boat and later Jesus comes to them on the water...*walking* on the water.

After the crowd finds them, we get to listen in on their conversation with Jesus.

I imagine it must have felt like pieces of a puzzle being interlocked. They knew about the manna from heaven, they had just felt the bread in their hands as they handed it out, and then the words spoken to Moses, "I am," now heard from Jesus' mouth.

"I AM the Bread of Life..."

Read John 6:25-40, 47-51

What does He mean when He says "I am the bread of life?"

What do you think the crowd and disciples thought when they heard this? What does it mean in your life that He is the bread of life?

We are desperate for light.

Sometimes I think the darkness is just too much.
We need a light.
We need The Light.

So when I read Jesus's words "I am the light of the world," I grip them tight like a flashlight in the dark of night.

He didn't say squint harder or just let your eyes adjust to darkness or scramble for another light source.

But He is the light.

And by His light I see everything else...

I see the world around me with clarity.

I see others with His compassion and love.

I see myself with His overflowing grace.

And most importantly, I see Him with wonder and awe.

But like Jesus often does, He goes further: "you are the light of the world." Me? You? The light of the world?

Honestly, I hardly understand this. But I don't think I have to, because I am not the source. He is. And I simply reflect Him. He is the sun, I am the moon.

What a joy and privilege to know Him and to reflect Him in a dark world.

So when life feels like too much, I look to Him, my source. His light illuminates the darkness. His light gives me clarity. His light lights my way home.

He rarely shines like a spotlight, illuminating the whole path. Instead He shines like a candle, illuminating just enough for the next step or decision. A spotlight doesn't require faith but candlelight does.

Trusting the Light of the world means living in total reliance on Him to see, *and*
trusting that the amount of light I have is enough.

Jesus,
show us Your light,
shine Your light on us that we may see You as You are,
give us discernment to walk away from darkness,
pour Your glorious light in and through us to give sight to all those around us,
illuminate Your truth.

Read the following Scriptures, making notes of all you learn about The Light. John 8:1-12, John 1:4-5, 1 John 1: 5-7

The Gate and the Good Shepherd / Day 20

One way I read and digest Scripture, is to begin with a list titled, "I Notice…:

This is a great way to begin to study and to be aware and NOTICE what the passage says.

Noticing, observing, paying attention to, and being aware of what is taking place around us and in us is not our default. In our culture we tend to skim, numb out, or be distracted, but noticing is a skill we have to practice.

We especially want to Notice when reading the narrative of Scripture - paying attention to the passage, to the people in the passage, to God, to us as we read, and to how the words infiltrate the rest of our life.

Spend some time in John 10.

In it you'll find two of Jesus' "I am" statements: "I am the Gate for the sheep." John 10:7,9 "I am the Good Shepherd." John 10:11,14

Make your own "I Notice…" list.

The Life / Day 21

How fitting that Jesus' declaration that He is the Resurrection and the Life is given to Martha just before He raises her brother, Lazarus, from the dead. He speaks these words to her grief. She probably did not grasp the profundity of His words until much later. Can you imagine her delight when the truth of His words settled deep into her soul?

Have His words settled deep into your soul as well?

Read John 11:1-45 while keeping in mind the Scripture below:

I am the way, the truth, and the life. No one comes to the Father but by Me. John 14:6

Jesus is

The Way to the Father

John 14:6 ...no one comes to the Father but by Me.

The Truth from the Father

John 12:49: For I did not speak on my own, but the Father who sent me commanded me to say all that I have spoken.

The Life with the Father

John 14:23 "If anyone loves me, he will obey my teaching. My Father will love him, and we will come to him and make our home with him.

How do you know Jesus is the resurrection and the life? How have you experienced Him as the way, the truth, and the life?

The True Vine / Day 22

Let's look at our last "I am" statement of Jesus today using a simple method that can be used for any passage.

Read the passage, ask these three questions and write your answers.

1. What do I learn about God (Father, Son, Spirit)?
2. What do I learn about myself?
3. What does this affect in my life?

John 15:1-8

"I am the true vine, and my Father is the gardener. He cuts off every branch in me that bears no fruit, while every branch that does bear fruit he prunes so that it will be even more fruitful. You are already clean because of the word I have spoken to you. Remain in me, as I also remain in you. No branch can bear fruit by itself; it must remain in the vine. Neither can you bear fruit unless you remain in me.
"I am the vine; you are the branches. If you remain in me and I in you, you will bear much fruit; apart from me you can do nothing. If you do not remain in me, you are like a branch that is thrown away and withers; such branches are picked up, thrown into the fire and burned. If you remain in me and my words remain in you, ask whatever you wish, and it will be done for you. This is to my Father's glory, that you bear much fruit, showing yourselves to be my disciples.

The Radiance of God's Glory / Day 23

Who do you say Jesus is?
This is the most important questions of our lives.

Hebrews 1:3 *The Son is the radiance of God's glory and the exact representation of his being, sustaining all things by his powerful word. After he had provided purification for sins, he sat down at the right hand of the Majesty in heaven.*

Colossians 2:9-10 tells us: For in Christ all the fullness of the Deity lives in bodily form, and in Christ you have been brought to fullness. He is the head over every power and authority.

Jesus is the radiance of God's glory.
Jesus is the exact representation of His being.
Jesus contains or possesses all the fullness of the Deity.
All we know about God is embodied in Jesus Christ.

Pause on this truth for a bit.

The Glorious, Unchanging and Consistent, Exalted, Holy, Eternal, Creator, Creative, Sovereign, Omnipotent, Omniscient, Omnipresent God…
born as a baby…
the fullness of God in flesh and blood…

Today, spend some time in the Amplified version of Philippians 2:6-11 below, and then answer these questions:

When we consider that Christ "possessed the fullness of the attributes which make God God" (AMP), what does that tell us about His heart, that He didn't cling to or "grasp" His exalted position and instead made Himself nothing"?

What does that show you about His heart for the world?

What does that show you about His heart for you?

The Amplified Version of Philippians 2:6-7:
[Jesus} Who, although being essentially one with God and in the form of God [possessing the fullness of the attributes which make God God], did not think this equality with God was a thing to be eagerly grasped or retained,
But stripped Himself [of all privileges and rightful dignity], so as to assume the guise of a servant (slave), in that He became like men and was born a human being.

Today spend your day bringing this request before Him, *"Lord, show me who you are. Give me eyes to see the radiance of Your glory."*

The Word / Day 24

We saw in yesterday's Scripture that God speaks through His Son. As the sun's heat radiates to every living thing, so the Father radiates His glory through the Son. All that the Father is - his heart, His character - pours forth through the Son. Want to know the Father? Look at the Son.

Hebrews 1:3 *The Son is the radiance of God's glory and the exact representation of his being, sustaining all things by his powerful word. After he had provided purification for sins, he sat down at the right hand of the Majesty in heaven.*

He not only shows us the Father, but He makes a way to the Father (John 14:6), intercedes to the Father (Romans 8:34), and invites us into His communion with the Father (John 14:23).

So, when John tells us Jesus is "the Word," it means more than He carries the Father's message, but that *He is* the Father's message.

Take the following Scriptures with you throughout the day. If you're able to, read one in the morning, one in the middle of the day, and the last one at the end of your day.

John 1:1 *In the beginning was the Word, and the Word was with God, and the Word was God.*

John 1:14 *The Word became flesh and made his dwelling among us. We have seen his glory, the glory of the one and only Son, who came from the Father, full of grace and truth.*

1 John 1:1 *That which was from the beginning, which we have heard, which we have seen with our eyes, which we have looked at and our hands have touched—this we proclaim concerning the Word of life.*

What wisdom, joy or comfort do you receive from the truth that Jesus is The Word?

Emmanuel / Day 25

They will call Him Emmanuel, which means God with us.
Matthew 1:23

When these words were first uttered, it was revolutionary.

God had been with His people, but this was different. He took on flesh, and as we read yesterday, the Word became flesh and made His dwelling among us (John 1:14).

Philippians 2: 6-8 *Who, being in very nature God, did not consider equality with God something to be used to his own advantage; rather, he made himself nothing by taking the very nature of a servant, being made in human likeness. And being found in appearance as a man, he humbled himself by becoming obedient to death—even death on a cross!*

God became one of us at the incarnation.

The living, breathing, fully human Jesus was with His disciples, with the sick, with the desperate, and even with His accusers.

It is this Emmanuel's voice, the voice of the God who is with us, we hear in John 15. Using the analogy of vines and branches, Jesus shares about the "with-ness" that would be the trademark of His kingdom. He knew this would be a clear picture of infinite truth to finite minds, an illustration of unseen spiritual realities.

Upon first hearing, they probably thought, "I guess He likes plants or something..." They didn't fully grasp the way life would work on the other side of the ascension, they didn't grasp the coming Spirit, and they certainly didn't grasp the profound truth of abiding.

"Emmanuel, God with us" was more than an announcement of God's visit at the birth of Christ and more than a commentary of Jesus' social life; it was the declaration that you and I can spend our days abiding in Him; an invitation to make our home in Him. As we go through life, we are not alone for He is our constant companion. This is a revolutionary intimacy.

At His crucifixion, it might have looked as if this new, profound "with-ness" was a temporary false hope, but what looked like defeat was actually accomplishing the very thing He came for:

"I will ask the Father, and he will give you another Helper to be with you forever. The Helper is the Spirit of truth. The people of the world cannot accept him, because they don't see him or know him. But you know him. He lives with you, and he will be in you." (John 14:15-17)

Spend time in Psalm 139 today.

Do you believe He is with you, in you, among you?

How does this affect you today?

The One in whom all of God's fullness dwells, the One by whom all the names and promises are fulfilled, and the One for whom we "live and move and have our being," is called

Man of Sorrow, acquainted with grief.

He is the exalted, victorious, overcoming Savior.
He knows the end of the story.
He knows victory is sure.
He knows how short our lives are.
He knows that all pain will one day be overshadowed by glory.
He knows how temporary our suffering is.
He knows how eternal the glory will be.
And yet.
He enters into our suffering.
He doesn't dismiss it. He doesn't bypass our grief. He doesn't ignore our pain. He doesn't shame us for struggling. He enters into it all.
Did you read that?
Jesus doesn't dismiss our suffering; He enters into it with us.
He knows how dark the dark nights are for us.
He knows the heartache of sickness and death.
He knows the despair of our wounds, neglect, abuse, and pain.
.

Recently a situation hurt my feelings. At first, I wanted to tell about it, post about it, and retaliate, until I went for a walk and the Lord kindly asked to be invited into it. I sensed Him saying, "Maybe this is where I'd like to work. You want to experience My supernatural healing of your heart, but you continue to marinate in anger and self-pity. My healing happens where there are wounds."

Could it be that our wounds (from traumatic abuse to hurt feelings, and everything in between) are the very places He wishes to be invited into?

.

I encourage you today. Sit with Him. Go into that figurative room where you've shoved all the hurts and barred the door and know your Emmanuel is there with you.

Read Isaiah 53 and then invite the One acquainted with grief into your grief today.

Friend / Day 27

Matthew 11:18-19 18 For John came neither eating nor drinking, and they say, 'He has a demon.' 19 The Son of Man came eating and drinking, and they say, 'Here is a glutton and a drunkard, a friend of tax collectors and sinners.' But wisdom is proved right by her deeds."

Jesus was first called a "friend of sinners" as an insult from the Pharisees:

how could the Messiah hang out with "those people?" who does he think he is living in such freedom, hanging out with sinners?

It's funny that the Pharisees had separate categories for themselves and for those who didn't follow their guidelines. And yet, when we read about His interactions with them, we find that they received His harshest rebuke. But to the "sinners," Jesus offered grace and restoration.

If the Pharisees could have seen the reality of their situation, they would have seen that the category included them.

When we stop comparing ourselves to each other and instead keep God's holiness in view, we find that we all qualify as "sinners." Thank God--that's who He came to redeem.

"On hearing this, Jesus said to them, "It is not the healthy who need a doctor, but the sick. I have not come to call the righteous, but sinners." Mark 2:17"

We must be careful when we delineate who is a sinner and who is not, because what we think might be justifying ourselves before the Lord is actually disqualifying us: He came for those of us who know we need a Savior.

He did not come to add a little extra goodness to an already good life.

He doesn't offer spiritual cold medicine, He offers resurrected life to the spiritually dead…of which we all, each of us, qualify.

Here's where this truth progresses from amazing to earth-shattering:

John 15:12-17 *My command is this: Love each other as I have loved you. Greater love has no one than this: to lay down one's life for one's friends. You are my friends if you do what I command. I no longer call you servants, because a servant does not know his master's business. Instead, I have called you friends, for everything that I learned from my Father I have made known to you. You did not choose me, but I chose you and appointed you so that you might go and bear fruit—fruit that will last—and so that whatever you ask in my name the Father will give you. This is my command: Love each other.*

Jesus calls us friends and then He further defines that by saying "friends know each other's business."

Not only does Jesus share Himself with us at salvation, but He shares His business with us. He lets us in on what He's doing, on His heart. He tells us what the Father tells Him. Does He have to do this? No. Could we be brought into the kingdom without knowing all His business? Yes.

So why, why does the Lord offer us this next-level-intimate-engaging kind of relationship?

It must be that you and I were made to know Him in this way. Were we made to serve Him? Yes, of course. Is He high and exalted and deserving of our highest honor and praise? Yes!

And yet, He shares Himself with us in the closest of ways. He tells us His master's business.

He calls us friends.

Wow.

.

Here are a few more Scriptures to sit with today.

"Lord, help us understand Your friendship."

Jeremiah 33:3 Call to me and I will answer you and tell you great and unsearchable things you do not know.'

Revelation 3:20 'Look! I stand at the door and knock. If you hear my voice and open the door, I will come in, and we will share a meal together as friends.

John 17:25-26 "Righteous Father, though the world does not know you, I know you, and they know that you have sent me. I have made you known to them, and will continue to make you known in order that the love you have for me may be in them and that I myself may be in them."

What aspect of Jesus' friendship stands out the most to you?

High Priest / Day 28

Jesus as our High Priest is something we could spend a lot of time studying. The role of the High Priest in the Old Testament, Jesus' fulfillment of that role, what that means for you and me…so much deep profound truth!

Before the Messiah came, God's presence was in the Most Holy Place. He was, in a sense, off limits, except for the High Priest who was allowed to enter once a year with many stipulations, to offer a blood sacrifice for the sins of the people. The Priest went before God on behalf of the people.

Priests go before God on behalf of the people; Prophets, speak to the people on behalf of God…Our Savior is Prophet, Priest, and King…as He represents God to us and us to before God, He also has all authority to rule and reign. Wow.

But now, our Savior has opened wide the Most Holy Place. Beginning with the ripped curtain at His death, Jesus has now made living in Him possible and we are allowed, urged even, to enter into the very presence of God.
You can almost hear the shout, "COME IN, DWELL WITH ME; ENTER IN AND STAY—ABIDE HERE."
He is ever-drawing, ever-wooing us to Himself. We simply enter by faith. We forsake (or forfeit) the magnitude of this gift when we remain "outside the veil," content to know about God, visit with Him from time to time, but not enter and remain within this hallowed place the blood of Christ opened for us.

We still belong to Him, our "anchor is still within the veil," but we are forfeiting what He has freely given us when we do not abide in and with Him. We may still think of Him a little or read His word, but the constancy of remaining is lacking. He has cleared the path, telling us that He is the way into the very throne room of God and we are often content to remain outside the rent veil, going about our daily routine, settling for shadows and substitutes while the life-giving power is found within, in Him.

What a truth! I am made clean, declared righteous, and invited to live in His presence. I have access to the Living God. The power over sin—to say no to those things that I can't seem to shake—is found there, the companionship that I've looked for all my life is there, the approval, the love—oh the love!, the healing, the glory—everything is there in His presence.

But most of all, God is there. The God who hand-knit me, the God who knows the intricate places of my heart better than I do, the God who has wooed me since childhood is there. How do we "take hold" of this benefit of being His child? How do we enter into His ongoing, perpetual, constant presence?

We enter by faith.

Surely this is what Jesus meant when He said, "I am the vine, you are the branches...remain in me..."

Does this mean that we live a "head in the clouds" Christianity? Are we supposed to "live in His presence" so much that we are unaware and unaffected by the rest of the world? Nope.

We don't escape the world, but we bring God's presence into the world...into our jobs, our families, conversations, relationships...

It's fine to retreat, after all, God is our refuge. But don't forget that the same God who said "enter in" also said "Go and tell, go and make..."

Read Hebrews 4:14-5:10 Make note of all you learn about Him as your High Priest.

What does it mean that Jesus goes to the Father on our behalf?

What does it mean that He is the High Priest?

What does it mean that He's your High Priest?

Sunday / Remember and Worship

Happy Sunday friends. Today, spend some time reviewing what you've learned so far during our time together. Look at your notes or review the posts and comments. Notice what has stood out to you over these last several days.

This week we're going to look at some of the Scriptures that tell us about Jesus' healings. And then next week will be Holy Week, and we'll look at the details of the days that led up to Jesus' crucifixion and resurrection.

Mark 2: 1-12 *A few days later, when Jesus again entered Capernaum, the people heard that he had come home. They gathered in such large numbers that there was no room left, not even outside the door, and he preached the word to them. Some men came, bringing to him a paralyzed man, carried by four of them. Since they could not get him to Jesus because of the crowd, they made an opening in the roof above Jesus by digging through it and then lowered the mat the man was lying on. When Jesus saw their faith, he said to the paralyzed man, "Son, your sins are forgiven." Now some teachers of the law were sitting there, thinking to themselves, "Why does this fellow talk like that? He's blaspheming! Who can forgive sins but God alone?" Immediately Jesus knew in his spirit that this was what they were thinking in their hearts, and he said to them, "Why are you thinking these things? Which is easier: to say to this paralyzed man, 'Your sins are forgiven,' or to say, 'Get up, take your mat and walk'? But I want you to know that the Son of Man has authority on earth to forgive sins." So he said to the man, "I tell you, get up, take your mat and go home." He got up, took his mat and walked out in full view of them all. This amazed everyone and they praised God, saying, "We have never seen anything like this!"*

The friends: these men carried the paralyzed man on the mat, went on the roof, made an opening in the roof, and lowered their friend down. They knew if they could just get their friend to Jesus, He would heal him. And they were right. I love where it says, "when Jesus saw their faith…" meaning "to stare at, behold… not just glanced at but saw and took it in."

Jesus took notice of their faith. I think of this when I'm praying for someone and bringing them to Jesus on a metaphorical mat, begging Jesus to heal and redeem them. Their faith moved Jesus to action; He took notice of their faith. Wow.

The man: We don't know much about him, but we do know he was paralyzed, and that he had dedicated friends.

If you were that man—what do you see, what do you notice? Are you embarrassed? Are you grateful for the sacrifice of your friends? Are you as certain as they are that healing is possible? Are you nervous that the homeowner will get ticked? Are you nervous Jesus will see you as an interruption? If I were the man on the mat, I would have wondered if Jesus would be annoyed? This huge crowd has gathered, Jesus is teaching, He is important…Who am I to interrupt?

But then the moment of all moments:

Take heart, son, your sins are forgiven.

Take heart, son…

Not only tolerated, but welcomed

Not just acknowledge, but seen

Not an acquaintance, but a term of endearment

Imagine it: you had been dependent on others for years, and now this Man pauses, welcomes you, sees you, speaks kindness to you, acknowledges your's and your friends' faith and then validates their risky move.

This moment changed this man's life physically, spiritually, and in every other way as well.

The grumblers: to say this man's sins were forgiven was blasphemy because only God can do that. But Jesus wasn't blaspheming against God because He was God. Jesus offered forgiveness first, showing that physical healing was secondary to spiritual healing. His physical healing illustrated what He was doing spiritually. Jesus made the connection here, not in a way their culture had incorrectly done by thinking physical trouble always had a direct spiritual cause (ie, sin caused sickness), but made the connection by giving the visual of what He did internally.

While you and I may not have all things in common with this man, we do have the spiritual need of forgiveness in common with him. Each of us has been rendered spiritually incapable to walk in new life, we each have needs beyond our ability to meet,

And we each need Jesus to welcome us, to see us, to speak kindness to us and to heal us. In every way.

"Get up" He told the man. Similar to His words to Lazarus: "come out" (John 11:43); to the man at the pool: "pick up your mat" (John 5:8); to the blind man: "go wash the mud off your eyes"(John 9:7).

It took faith to carry the man to Jesus; it took faith for the man to cooperate; *and* it took faith for this man to take his mat and go home.

It takes faith for us to pray, to ask for Him to heal others, and to heal us, *and* it also takes faith to walk in the healing Jesus gives us. How silly it would have been for the man to stay on his mat.

Jesus offers us healing, the question is have we taken our mat and walked?

.

Do you know Jesus sees you? When He sees you, does He notice your faith? Who are you bringing to Him?

In the comments:

How does knowing Jesus sees you affect you today?

Be Clean! / 30

While Jesus was in one of the towns, a man came along who was covered with leprosy. When he saw Jesus, he fell with his face to the ground and begged him, "Lord, if you are willing, you can make me clean." Jesus reached out his hand and touched the man. "I am willing," he said. "Be clean!" And immediately the leprosy left him. Luke 5:12-13

If I had to give the passage above a title, it would be:

~The Desperation of a Sick Man and the Willingness of Jesus~

Put yourself in the story, let's practice NOTICING...
–First as an observer: you're sitting, watching this all take place. What goes through your mind.
–Then as the leper: what is that experience like?
...
What does it do to a man who had been sick, declared unclean, and sidelined from life to now hear the Man, who had a reputation for healing others, now tell you
"...I am willing"
What does it do to a man to not only hear those words, but to also be touched...to be healed with the very thing the disease stole from him...
...It heals him. It heals his physical body and it heals him from the destruction the illness caused the rest of his life.
What does it do to a man to receive back his dignity?
...The face of Jesus, the words of Jesus, the touch of Jesus all told this man he wasn't nothing, he wasn't discarded, he wasn't forgotten, he was worth Jesus' time.
He could have healed the leper from a distance. He had healed with a word before, but in this instance, His "be clean" was coupled with a touch. We read about others who were

healed from a distance so Jesus was clearly making a statement with His touch.

This man may not have been a "first hearer" of one of Jesus' profound teachings (like we've discussed before), but consider what teaching the man and his healing personifies. Like the leper, we too were separated from God, from others, from LIFE. We were "unclean" and "untouchable"...

Jesus' touch teaches a clear truth: He came to enter into all the mess, the brokenness, the sin, the sickness, the social destruction our brokenness has caused. He didn't come to say the state of our hearts, minds, bodies, and our world was ok...He came to enter in, to heal from within...so we would no longer be the outcast but invited to enter into His presence. And like I shared in our video: we don't have to ruminate on "the mess," but we can marinate in His restoration and glory!

I love Jesus' disregard for the "rules of cleanliness" knowing He was the only One who could make any of us clean.

What does it do to a man...what does it do to a woman...to encounter the Healer, the One to whom all sickness must bow?

What does it do to a man or woman to hear these words: I am willing?

What does it do to a man or woman to feel the restorative touch for which you've longed?

What does it do to a man or woman to receive back the dignity of being a precious child of the Living God?

Take Heart, Daughter / Day 31

Matthew 9:18-26
18 While he was saying this, a synagogue leader came and knelt before him and said, "My daughter has just died. But come and put your hand on her, and she will live." 19 Jesus got up and went with him, and so did his disciples. 20 Just then a woman who had been subject to bleeding for twelve years came up behind him and touched the edge of his cloak. 21 She said to herself, "If I only touch his cloak, I will be healed." 22 Jesus turned and saw her. "Take heart, daughter," he said, "your faith has healed you." And the woman was healed at that moment. 23 When Jesus entered the synagogue leader's house and saw the noisy crowd and people playing pipes, 24 he said, "Go away. The girl is not dead but asleep." But they laughed at him. 25 After the crowd had been put outside, he went in and took the girl by the hand, and she got up. 26 News of this spread through all that region.

"Put your hand on her and she will live"
"If I only touch His cloak, I will be healed."
Stories like this bring up something a friend once said to me, "I know He can heal; I just don't know if He will." That's a legitimate thought isn't it? Because we all know people who Jesus didn't heal. Or maybe we should say, He didn't heal them how we thought, but gave them ultimate healing by bringing them home to be with Him.
Passages like this make me think, "I just need to have more faith." But it can't be lack of faith that always prohibits earthly healing. Jesus even says faith the size of a mustard seed is effective.

It's important, when reading Scripture, that we don't bypass these hard questions. And it's important that we don't simplify the mystery of God to a simple one-liner or explanation. It's ok that we don't quite understand, it reminds us that right now we know in part, then we will know fully."

It's also important that the questions a passage brings up don't distract us from the beautiful truth that is clear.

In this story, we see the Jesus who is responsive and attentive.

He got up to go with the man to heal his daughter.

And He turned and saw the bleeding woman.

He is on His way to heal a daughter, but then a bold woman touches his cloak. Surely she wasn't certain what His response would be, but she was desperate.

Then, like we're told at the beginning of this chapter, the moment of all moments:

Jesus turned and saw her.

Take heart, daughter, your faith has healed you.

Take heart, daughter...

One who would've been considered unclean is now commended for her bold reach.

Not just acknowledge, but seen

Not an acquaintance, but a term of endearment

This moment changed this woman's life physically, spiritually, and in every other way as well.

Mark tells us *But Jesus kept looking around to see who had done it. 33 Then the woman, knowing what had happened to her, came and fell at his feet and, trembling with fear, told him the whole truth. 34 He said to her, "Daughter, your faith has healed you. Go in peace and be freed from your suffering."(Mark 5:32-34)*

As you watch the Savior interact with this woman, as you see Him seeing her, what do you notice?

Do you see the thread of this chapter?

The threads of faith, desperation, and the attuned eye of the Savior?

Friend, do you see this thread in your life?

If so, how does this affect the way you see others around you?

Do You Want to Get Well? / Day 32

In John 9, we read of a man born blind who asks Jesus, "are you willing?" and today we will read of Jesus' question to a paralyzed man, "do you want to get well?"

Jesus' willingness and our desire - two essential ingredients to healing…and two ingredients to our spiritual healing as well.

Is He willing to heal our souls? And do we want to be well?

He's proven His willingness and power by what we are celebrating during this season – His willingness to go to the cross on our behalf and His power displayed in the resurrection.

Do we want to get well?

Do we want to experience true soul-health? Do we want the restoration He offers? And when the question comes, do we offer an excuse as to why we are the way we are? We pray that God would transform us from the inside out, but oftentimes we resist what He's doing on our insides and want Him to skip to fixing our outsides.

If His answer to my request for healing were "get up and walk," what would my response be?

Read John 5:1-18. Write the phrases that stand out to you.

Lord, we ask for Your powerful, supernatural soul healing. We want to be well. Transform us from the inside out.

Do You Believe I am Able? / Day 33

Matthew 9:27-34 tells us of a time when Jesus restored the sight of two men and the speech of another.
Don't miss the symbolism that Jesus restored sight and speech.
It is always the enemy's hope that we will be blinded to God, to ourselves, and to those around us and that we will feel like we need to keep quiet. His desire is to diminish our ability to experience, discern, and distinguish the world around us.

Our senses were given to us by God to take in all that is around us. Think about it, food didn't have to have taste, flowers didn't have to smell, music and art didn't have to appeal to us (or technically didn't have to exist in the first place, but I know most creatives would disagree).

The way we live in this world and experience what is around us is set up by God Himself. Tasting a watermelon is one way we experience His handiwork…and a practical way we understand how God's divine creation and man's collaboration work together.

When we see the magnitude of the sunset or the smallness of a newborn's pinky toe, we can't help but lose our breath in His divine creativity, grandeur, and detailed attention.

The enemy, however, would rather paint all of life in a dull gray. He would rather us live numb and unaware of the beauty around us, in us, and waiting for us in eternity.

The enemy will always seek to steal, kill, and destroy. He wants to "shut us down."

But God gives abundant LIFE. And life is meant to be lived!

Are you living the abundant life God has plopped into your lap or are you forfeiting it and in essence collaborating with the enemy by living a life that is "shut down and checked out?"

Imagine if the leper stayed in the isolated wilderness
Imagine if the bleeding woman continued living her life as if she were not healed and declared clean
Imagine if the Ruler's daughter stayed on her bed
Imagine if the paralytic stayed on his mat

Even as I type this, I'm reminded of so many who have "checked out" and have decided to play it safe.

Read Matthew 9:27-34. Spend some time today asking the Lord if you have forfeited His abundance or if you're living freely in His power and healing.

Tomorrow we'll wrap up our time looking at Jesus' healings, and then Sunday will begin Holy Week. Let's ask Jesus to shepherd us and draw us near as we prepare for Easter.

Lazarus, Come Out! / Day 34

As we read about Lazarus, we're told, "Mary is the same one who poured perfume on the Lord and wiped his feet with her hair."
Lazarus is sick, and when they send word to Jesus, they identify their brother as "the one You love."
It's as if John wanted us to know, this wasn't just anyone's brother –this was Mary's brother, and Jesus loved Him.

Upon first read, it might look like John is just showing us that these people were close with Jesus. But he includes it to show that Jesus' delay wasn't careless neglect. His delay had a purpose. There were other times Jesus went to help or heal immediately, but now we read:
Now Jesus loved Martha and her sister and Lazarus. So when he heard that Lazarus was sick, he stayed where he was two more days...
Maybe John wanted us to see that Jesus' love does not mean He excludes hard things.
In His delay, or in His "no," there is no neglect, but love.

It's easy to read this story, and since we know Lazarus would be raised, to accept His delay as a commitment to a bigger purpose and story being told. But Mary and Martha had no such hindsight. They were living *in* the story. They asked Jesus to come and help "the one He loved," and then they waited...
You and I, as we are living *in* our story, have no such hindsight either. We pray and ask and wait. Sometimes we see His answer, and sometimes we don't. When Jesus "waits" or when His answer is no, we are forced to look at the ground

beneath our feet to see just how strong it is. Do we stand on assumptions, on platitudes, on optimism... or do we stand on the very strong, sometimes mysterious, rock which is the truth of our good God and the eternal hope He's promised.

Jesus tells them that this was for God's glory: so that through the resurrection of Lazarus, they would believe and see His power.

"When Mary reached the place where Jesus was and saw him, she fell at his feet and said, "Lord, if you had been here, my brother would not have died."

Once again, Mary is at Jesus' feet. This time she is weeping and heartbroken.
Jesus is deeply moved and then,
"Jesus wept."
Jesus, God incarnate, shed real, gut-wrenching, tears. He knew the purpose and He knew the outcome, and yet, He wept.

Friend, when you weep, Jesus weeps alongside you. Does He know the ultimate story? Does He know that eternity is so so long and life is so so short? Yes and yes. And yet, He weeps with those who weep.
And then the words that ring throughout the ages,

"Lazarus, Come out!"

Wow. What a visual to the truth He had just graciously given to Martha, "I am the resurrection."

When Lazarus's physical body was resurrected, all of his bodily systems were brought back to life as well.
His stilled heart began beating,
His lungs took a gasp,
His stagnated blood began flowing.
His resurrection affected every part of him.

Just as a bodily resurrection has countless ramifications, the spiritual resurrection Jesus offers us has far-reaching effects as well.

And as He calls us forth, from death to life, He also calls forth every part of us:
He *has* resurrected us and He *is* resurrecting us.
How has He resurrected you? What effect has He had in your life?

Read John 11:1-44, taking note of words and phrases to take with you today. Ask God to show you the ramifications the resurrection has had on your life.

Hosanna! Holy Week: Palm Sunday

See, your king comes to you,
righteous and victorious,
lowly and riding on a donkey
Zechariah 9:9

The Triumphant Entry is an interesting title for Jesus' arrival into Jerusalem. Sure, the crowd exclaims, "Hosanna, blessed is He who comes in the name of the Lord. Blessed is the King…"today, but in a few short days that same crowd will call for His death, "crucify Him" and then hang Him on a cross to suffer a criminal's death.

Doesn't sound very triumphant, does it?

Especially when we read that the very definition of triumph is "the processional entry of a victorious general." Triumph comes after the victory is won.

But this man was a different kind of king, ushering in a different kind of kingdom. He came in triumph because the victory was sure. We could even say His triumphant entry wasn't just His entry into the city, but it was His entry into the last phase of His mission: His suffering. What does it look like to triumphantly enter into suffering? Jesus shows us.

He came in humility and peace, not because His Father's attitude was resigned toward sin and suffering, but because His victory was won since the foundation of the world (Revelation 13:8).

What looked like defeat was part of a cosmic victory that changed the lives of men, women, children from all nations for generations back and generations forward, including yours and mine.

He enters Jerusalem on a donkey, humble and offering peace. He enters to the throng of excitement and will continue all the way to the cross, giving His life in our place to accomplish the victory that would change everything. He came in triumph then, and He comes to us in triumph now. His victory has been accomplished for us, in us, and yes even through us.

Lord, even when apparent defeat is staring us in the face, teach us how to live in your victory today.

Read the passage below. What stands out to you about His triumphant entry?

John 12:12-16 *The next day the great crowd that had come for the festival heard that Jesus was on his way to Jerusalem. They took palm branches and went out to meet him, shouting, "Hosanna!" "Blessed is he who comes in the name of the Lord! Blessed is the king of Israel!" Jesus found a young donkey and sat on it, as it is written, "Do not be afraid, Daughter Zion; see, your king is coming, seated on a donkey's colt." At first his disciples did not understand all this. Only after Jesus was glorified did they realize that these things had been written about him and that these things had been done to him.*

Welcome this King into your life, welcome him into the recesses of your heart, welcome Him into your thoughts, your affections. Welcome him into your celebrations, your relationships…

Welcome your Savior King.

Clearing the Temple / Day 35 / Holy Monday

The Monday before Jesus crucifixion is written about in Matthew 21:12-19. We find Jesus clearing the temple and cursing the fig tree.

Both scenarios give us another aspect of the person and work of Jesus. We know Jesus was full of grace and truth and He loved sacrificially. And yet, we find times like these when He was angry or indignant. Holding these things together helps us have a more full, accurate understanding of who He is. We tend to focus on one aspect of His character and exclude some of His other characteristics. Here we find injustice, oppression, or deceit was not ok with Him. We find His frustration when things were not as they were meant to be.

Many of us have been taught or assumed that emotions are not godly. Jesus shows us a different picture. Of course, we are not led by our emotions, but we can express our God-given emotion when necessary. We *should* be bothered when others are wronged; we *should* take action if we are able when someone is mistreated. Inconvenient? Usually. Is there a risk of being misunderstood? Jesus' life declares a loud "yes." However, if love, by definition, is sacrificial, and if we are to seek the good of others regardless of the cost to ourselves, we must not dismiss emotion and action as ungodly. Instead let us remember Jesus' words in John 15:13, "greater love has no one than this, that He lay down His life for His friends."

Prayerfully read Matthew 21:12-19, asking the Lord to cause your heart to more closely align with His.

Jesus is Anointed / Day 36 / Holy Tuesday

John 12:1-11

Six days before the Passover, Jesus came to Bethany, where Lazarus lived, whom Jesus had raised from the dead. Here a dinner was given in Jesus' honor. Martha served, while Lazarus was among those reclining at the table with him. Then Mary took about a pint of pure nard, an expensive perfume; she poured it on Jesus' feet and wiped his feet with her hair. And the house was filled with the fragrance of the perfume.
But one of his disciples, Judas Iscariot, who was later to betray him, objected, "Why wasn't this perfume sold and the money given to the poor? It was worth a year's wages." He did not say this because he cared about the poor but because he was a thief; as keeper of the money bag, he used to help himself to what was put into it.
"Leave her alone," Jesus replied. "It was intended that she should save this perfume for the day of my burial. **You will always have the poor among you, but you will not always have me." Meanwhile a large crowd of Jews found out that Jesus was there and came, not only because of him but also to see Lazarus, whom he had raised from the dead. So the chief priests made plans to kill Lazarus as well, for on account of him many of the Jews were going over to Jesus and believing in him.

She was being scolded to stop, risking embarrassment, and being misunderstood.

"Why this waste?"

One of the lessons we learn from Mary's beautiful act is this:

She was simply responding to her heart's devotion by pouring the perfume on Jesus, but what she probably didn't know was that her act was preparing Him for something coming just a few days later. The body of a criminal wasn't typically prepared for burial, but as God often does, in His divine sovereignty, He used her simple and profound act of devotion to prepare Jesus' body for His death.

I wonder how often God uses a simple act of devotion or obedience, superintends the details, and causes it to become something that is exponentially more meaningful or powerful than we ever anticipated.

We know to Judas, Jesus was worth only a few pieces of silver; but to Mary, Jesus' worth was incalculable.

May we remember that when we live out of an extravagant love for our extravagant God, we will be misunderstood. The way we give and spend ourselves—our time, our money, and our giftedness will be questioned and discredited as foolish.

I'm reminded of David's words in 2 Samuel 24:24, *I will not give to God that which costs me nothing.*

May we each offer to God our costly, extravagant devotion, just as He offered us His costly, extravagant devotion on the cross.

Betrayal / Day 37 / Holy Wednesday

Holy Wednesday is sometimes called "Spy Wednesday" because it is believed it was the day Judas conspired to betray Jesus.

Matthew puts the following passage right after telling of Mary pouring perfume on Jesus in an extravagant display of devotion and love (we read about her on Monday). Matthew didn't tell these two stories chronologically, but he placed them side by side to use contrast to teach us.

Matthew 26:14-16 *Then one of the twelve, whose name was Judas Iscariot, went to the chief priests and said, "What will you give me if I deliver him over to you?" And they paid him thirty pieces of silver. And from that moment he sought an opportunity to betray him.*

To Mary, Jesus was worth everything.

To Judas and the religious officials, Jesus was worth 30 pieces of silver.

To Mary, her sacrifice caused her to ask, what can I give?

To Judas, his greed asked the question, what can I get?

To Mary, Jesus was beautiful.

To Judas, Jesus was useful.

The woman's heart overflowed in praise.

Judas' heart was concerned with profit.

What else do you learn by looking at the contrast between Judas and Mary?

Lord, capture our hearts to live in extravagant devotion to you.

It was just before the Passover Festival. Jesus knew that the hour had come for him to leave this world and go to the Father. Having loved his own who were in the world, he now showed them the full extent of His love. John 13:1

He knew it was time. He had gone the distance with His disciples, teaching, transforming, and training. And now.

*having loved His own…***He now showed them the full extent of His love.**

Other translations of this verse say, "He now showed them the full extent of His love…He loved them to the uttermost…He loved them to the end."

All that came next was an answer to the question: "How much does He love us?"

Jesus washes their feet, gives them bread and wine to symbolize His body and blood, Satan enters Judas who then leaves to institute the betrayal, and then:

Love each other as I have loved you.

Whew, what a progression.

Maundy is short for the Latin word which means mandate or command. And what is the command today is known for?

A new commandment I give to you, that you love one another: just as I have loved you, you also are to love one another" John 13:34.

Jesus takes the command to love deeper than before by telling them to love as He loves: love regardless of the worth or response, love sacrificially, love wholeheartedly.

It's interesting to think that His main command was to love like He loves.

In a world with a twisted view of love, Jesus says, Love like I love. Watch what I'm doing. Learn from Me. This is love.

I'm reminded of John's definition of love in 1 John 4:10: *This is love: not that we loved God, but that he loved us and sent his Son as an atoning sacrifice for our sins.*

His sacrificial love is the plumb line.

Today we get to sit with the passage, John 13, from which I took the name for our Lent study: The Full Extent of His Love.

Prayerfully read the chapter four times and each time begin with the corresponding prayer and focus listed below.

1. Jesus, what did you feel?
2. Jesus, show me your heart.
3. Jesus, give me a view of your love.
4. Jesus, show me your heart for me.

We Are People of the Cross. / Day 39 / Good Friday

We are people of the cross.

We are people who remember the death of a man because we know He wasn't just a man.

We are people who don't turn away from the agony of Friday because we know the glory of Sunday.

We are people who see beauty in the paradox of God in human vesture nailed to a tree.

We are people who return to the cross again and again because it's on this cross that our guilt was exchanged, our redemption was secured, and our freedom was won.

We are people who know that suffering is not the end of the story, but the fertile ground for the miracle of new life.

He is the Savior who, though Creator of all, made Himself nothing.

He is the Savior who was betrayed for pocket change and questioned by small men.

He is the Savior who sat with sinners and rebuked the self-righteous.

He is the Savior who spoke healing with a word but touched the leper.

He is the Savior who fulfilled the promises and gave substance to the shadows.

He is the Savior who is now exalted on the throne that we still try to claim.

He is the Savior who, at the simple sound of His name, all knees will bow and all tongues will confess He is Lord.

We are people who cling to the cross because it's on this cross that our broken, sinful, questioning, wandering, fickle hearts collide with God's holy, exalted, eternal, extravagant sacrifice.

He is the Savior who showed us that death precedes resurrection and dark night precedes morning mercy.

.

Sit with John 19 today. Pause and remember His sacrifice.

Write a prayer to the Savior.

Silent Saturday / Day 40 / Silent Saturday

Friday was devastating, Sunday was miraculous. But Saturday. Saturday was quiet. The Saturdays of our souls are always marked with quiet questions, tears of confusion, examination of what we always assumed, recounting the past again and again.

Perhaps when darkness seems to be winning, God is doing the most work. Preparation for new life never looks promising. Until it is.

Perhaps when God is silent, we should turn our face to who He is and let grief do its beautiful work. There is a nearness to Him that isn't experienced any other way. The hope of Sunday is an assurance that the grave isn't the end of the story. It wasn't for Him and it isn't for you.

Today is one of waiting...

Matthew 27: 57-66 *As evening approached, there came a rich man from Arimathea, named Joseph, who had himself become a disciple of Jesus. Going to Pilate, he asked for Jesus' body, and Pilate ordered that it be given to him. Joseph took the body, wrapped it in a clean linen cloth, and placed it in his own new tomb that he had cut out of the rock. He rolled a big stone in front of the entrance to the tomb and went away. Mary Magdalene and the other Mary were sitting there opposite the tomb. The next day, the one after Preparation Day, the chief priests and the Pharisees went to Pilate. "Sir," they said, "we remember that while he was still alive that deceiver said, 'After three days I will rise again.' So give the order for the tomb to be made secure until the third day. Otherwise, his disciples may come and steal the body*

*and tell the people that he has been raised from the dead.
This last deception will be worse than the first."
"Take a guard," Pilate answered. "Go, make the tomb as
secure as you know how." So they went and made the tomb
secure by putting a seal on the stone and posting the guard.*

And then…silence, waiting…

What do you learn about the time in between Good Friday
and Resurrection Sunday? What about you, have you had any
of those in between times lately? What does faithful waiting
look like?

Why do you think there was a day between the crucifixion and
the resurrection in God's plan?

We Are People of the Empty Tomb / Easter Sunday

We are people of the empty tomb.

We are people who put Him on the cross, who laid Him in the tomb, and who weren't so sure until we encountered Him as the Risen One.

We are people who have heard His words when we were in that confining tomb, "come out!"

We are people who know our own waywardness, but His pursuit has won every time.

We are people who sometimes still visit the familiar grave even though it's empty, it's been conquered, and He's not there.

We are people who have the hope of the empty tomb telling us suffering will one day reveal healing, doubt will be transformed to faith, and death will yield to life.

We are people who can remember the agony, because the joy has far outweighed every ounce of it, (already and not yet!).

We are people who never tire of the story: His story, our story, and where our two stories collide.

We are people who remember the story, people who love the story!

We are people who tell the story, to you, to them, and to ourselves.

He is the Savior who lowered Himself and came near, went lower still to the grave, only to rise again to his exalted rightful place, and He's invited us on the same journey: death with Him and new life in Him.

He is the Savior who we cannot fashion into our own image, making Him understandable and agreeable, but instead must surrender to His profound mystery.

He is the Savior who didn't fit in the box they put Him in, and all our attempts to do the same will fail.

He is the Savior who battled evil and won and who conquered death in all its forms.

He is the Savior, the Living, ever-present King of kings and not just an insightful man with good ideas.

He is the Savior who now perpetually encounters the dead places in you and me, takes them to the cross and then the grave and then raises something new and living in their place.

We are people of the empty tomb, who no longer have destruction in our future, but glory.

.

Spend time in Matthew 28 and 1 Corinthians 15 today.

Abba Father, Your goodness is astounding. You gave us Your Son to redeem us and Your Spirit to guide us. You have created us, wooed us, and restored us. You have rescued us from darkness, and brought us into Your kingdom of life and light. Oh, may we never get over Your goodness and grace. In the strong and sufficient name of Your Son, Amen.

If you'd like more information on past and future studies, you can email me at heathergrantharrison@yahoo.com
Thank you for reading and sharing this journey together.
What a gift!
Xoxo,
hh

Made in the USA
Monee, IL
14 February 2023

27787807R00059